GROWING LOVE

Published 2021
Authored by Inela Salkic

A collection of poems written about my experiences with love, heartbreak, growth, and everything in between.
Cheers to 25 years of life.

One day it just hits you.

That you cannot continue to water the flowers of a
relationship on your own.
While your pitcher is almost entirely empty trying to
maintain the beauty of the field
Theirs is just about full.
Do they not care about the flowers?
Do they not see how much they enhance everything
around them?
What happens when you no longer have water left?
And the flowers die.
And everything all of a sudden *looks ugly*.
They can start to water the flowers now.
Now that they have seen how detrimental their
negligence has been.
But it will be no use.
What once was, cannot be revived, cannot be restored
to its pure beauty.
Don't tell yourself
They did not know, they did not have time, they could
not give.
They knew but only you gave.

For a moment

You feel okay
You pick yourself up and drag yourself out the door
You forget everything that is going on
You tell yourself today will be a good day
And it is.

You hold on to that shred of hope they give you

You cling on to the memories
You tell yourself things are good
I do not want to overbear
I do not want to be a burden
But why do you see
Someone giving you what you give in return
Someone being genuinely happy you are alive
Someone loving you
As a burden?
You deserve more, my love.

Wednesdays were particularly hard.

~~Do~~ what makes you happy

What makes your heart sing
What makes you feel like the sun is shining just for you
today
Don't look back.

Live with compassion

With kindness
Empathy
Always be good
Even when it is difficult
Even when the world gives you every reason not to
Even to those who are undeserving
Because that is what makes you, you.
And you are special.

You can choose to heal

You can choose to grow
To learn from all the bad you have been dealt
To appreciate the good
And move on.

And in that moment

You were free
You loved yourself
And embraced every tiny flaw you had
You took control
And you were happy
I liked that look for you.

Did you ever make it to Boston?

Did you stop by that cute little donut shop you loved so
much
And order one of each flavor
Did you walk your dog and enjoy the fresh air during
your favorite season
Ride your bike
Bake your famous (to-me) cookies
Read your book
Sing your heart out to our favorite song
Did you stargaze until you fell asleep tangled in your
blankets?
I hope you did, my love.
And I hope for a minute, you thought of me.

While you think you may have lost everything

In the depths of pain
We find the most important thing
Ourselves.

And if they must go

You must let them.

Sometimes we get too caught up in our own shit.

And by far the thing I loved most about you

Was that you were never afraid to be you.

I think who we end up with

Depends on us
Our actions
Our growth
The paths we take
What we choose to allow and what we reject

There is something quite special about those

Who find themselves caring more
In every situation they are put in
And they are broken down
They are purple and blue
They long for reciprocation
For consideration
They do not receive
Yet it is not in their soul to not care
As much as they can try to.

You walk this earth

Convincing yourself that you do not owe anyone
anything
You come and go as you please
You only think of yourself and never of how your
actions affect those who care about you
Everything is you you you.
How freeing of the mind to be so selfish
To not care about the damage you inflict.
And if it breaks me to care and give to others
I will give my all
I will choose to be broken
Because I never want to be like you.

I could fill a room with your silence

Why won't you tell me what I so desperately want to hear?

Regardless of how many times you show someone

how good you are for them
If they aren't willing to see it
You will never succeed
And that is not a weight you should carry.

That tight feeling in your chest

Overthinking every conversation
Every action
Breathe
Know that you are doing your best
Give yourself the compassion you give others
Breathe

I hope that when you have bad days

When you feel like you have no purpose
When you feel like everything you do is not good
enough
You remember all the hearts you've touched
All the laughs you've shared with the people who mean
the most to you
All the people's lives you've added so much value to
Just by being you
Because that is what is important, my love.

~~Do~~ not settle

You deserve it all
It may seem like it is never coming
And things only seem to ever fall apart
But you must love you enough
Until someone can love you just as much

One of the saddest things is seeing them do

everything for someone else
But they couldn't even do the bare minimum for you
You did not imagine what you shared
It was mutual
But ultimately
People do things for who they want
Unfortunately sometimes we're not that person
And we don't understand why
That does not reflect on us
It is not telling of who we are
That person just isn't right for us.

I did miss you of course

But I also missed peace
I missed the version of me I lost
Trying so hard to be the version of me that you wanted

We can only rebuild so many times

Until the foundation is completely lost
There is no home for you here.

So cry.

Let it out.

Remember that it is not your job to fix people.

I know how hard it is

You miss them
And that's okay
And maybe you feel better with them than without
them
But at this time
Things just aren't right
Don't lose out on the present trying to force it
Don't lose out, waiting for *them*
Live in the moment
Things will fall into place
The future is uncertain
Who will come and who will go
But you my love, must focus on the person who is
always there
You.

You grew tired

Tired of making space in your heart for someone new
again
Tired of repairing the damage the last one did
Tired of breaking down your walls
Just to build them ten times higher the next time
around
You grew tired

You would always wipe the tears off someone's face

Even if that person was the cause of your own
Because you knew pain
You and pain were knit so tight
And you did not want anyone else to feel that way

And if you have become a better person

Grew from your bad habits
Let go of that which does not serve you
Learned from your mistakes
Lived with genuine intentions and the best of motives
You have made it further than you know
Keep going.

Maybe I just wanted to be with you

Even if I knew it was temporary
Because for a small moment in time
You heart was my home
And mine was yours
And that was simply beautiful.

I made the mistake of jumping in

Too deep
Too quickly
I can't hold myself up in the deep end much longer.
I'm drowning.
Aren't you going to save me?

While we had to part

I will always cherish the moments we shared
Because in that time
You needed my light like I needed yours.
I hope you are no longer in the dark, my love.

Of course you are allowed to expect in return

everything it is that you give.
But not everyone is as pure as you, my love.

If someone has shown you time and time again

What kind of person they are
Please do not keep letting them into your life
You're only perpetuating a cycle of hurt for yourself
They don't feel as much as you do
They run on their own terms
And only want you when it's convenient for them
So they will be fine coming in and out of your life
But my love, you will be destroyed.
Because you feel *everything*
And you feel it with every ounce of your being
Please close the door on that chapter.
There are better stories to be written.

Life is easier when you see things for what they are

Instead of creating your own narratives
Do not villainize yourself trying to portray someone
else in a better light.

Sometimes

We want so badly to be loved
That we overlook the part where they are not at all our
person.

In the end, you are the only one living your life

So make sure that you do what is best for you
What is it that will make you happy?
At peace?
Chase that.

Maybe one day we will cross paths again

On a rainy day in San Francisco
And you'll tell me all about how happy you are
And I'll be happy for you, my love.

In the mess of all our feelings

Blue
Red
Yellow
Violet
A beautiful picture was painted.

We chased after our cab in the pouring rain

Laughing about it
Lights gleaming on the New York City street
Listening to our favorite song
And you gently kissed my hand
Leaning your head on mine
So happy to just be with one another
Where did that go?

You always feel bad

You always want to explain yourself
So that nobody thinks badly of you
So that you make sure no one is hurt by you
Because you'd never want to hurt anyone
You try and you over-do it
To the point where it's breaking you
Trying to make them understand
Sometimes people just don't want to understand, my love.
You did what you could
You laid your heart out on your sleeve
Stop overthinking so much
It shouldn't be this hard.
As many times as you can say something
In as many different ways as you can say it
It's always going to fall on deaf ears with someone who doesn't want to understand.

So take your time

Cry if you need to
You don't always have to be strong
You are allowed to feel
Sad
Angry
Worn out
And all the other emotions
Just as much as you are allowed to feel happy
We're always told happy emotions are pretty
Happy emotions are the only normal ones
The ones we should always have
But we are human
We are multifaceted
We deserve to feel how we feel.

Our worst experiences can make us that much more

grateful for our best ones.
In fact, they can make our best experiences feel even
better.
Remember that when you're feeling down.
There's better to come.

I look back at how happy you made me

And that's all I ever wanted, forever.

I'm sorry that you've been hurt

So hurt that you now fear love
That you've lost hope
That you can't trust again
But please
When the right person comes along
And shows you everything you've been missing
And treats you how you know you deserve to be
treated
Please don't ruin a good thing by being scared
Don't run
Please try to let them in
I know you don't want to be heartbroken again
But if we don't try
We won't find what we searched so hard for
Protect yourself, but know that everyone won't hurt
you.

As much as you want to work on things

Talk things out
Fight for it
Sometimes silence and moving on is the best choice.

Take care of yourself.

Of all the love I shared

Ours felt most genuine
The most real
But it stung the most when you left, too.

Sometimes I just wish things weren't so hard.

I replay that night in June

All the stars lit up the night sky
And all you could look at was me
Like I meant everything to you
And maybe in that moment I did
I wish I could freeze time.

Hold people accountable

Time passing is *not* an apology
Remember that when you are giving someone
a second chance.
Because people *do* make mistakes
But if you are willing to hear someone out and let them
back into your life after they hurt you
The least that they owe you is a goddamn "I'm sorry."

It's not that hard to be honest with people

With your intentions
With what you want
With what you expect
With how you feel.
Let's be honest.

Sometimes I wish we never met

Because I could avoid crying about you for 3 days
straight
I could avoid hoping that this would finally be the one
I could've lived life just as I was doing
But I guess things don't work that way
I just wish endings weren't so sad.

I know you're hurt

But please don't hurt me in return because you
couldn't do what was necessary for us
Please don't hurt me because you're upset I'm letting
things go
I have to do what's best for me
I do not want to beg to be loved.

It's hard not to compare the different kinds of love

we've experienced
Each love is different
Of course there will be similarities in situations and in
the people we choose to be with
But do not ever stay
Just because someone is better than the others
Or because you think you won't find someone as good
as them again
Or because you are lonely
Stay because you are loved
Stay because you are getting all that you need
Stay because you are happy
Stay because that person feels *right*.

Make sure that there's an equal effort

That you aren't burning yourself out
Trying to love someone
And not getting the same back
Because you know you deserve that love
And it will come.

Sometimes we don't get the closure we want

We don't get a conversation
We don't get an answer
Reasons
Explanations

Their actions speak, if they do not
Pay attention to that
They chose to leave didn't they?

Was any of it real?

It hurts to think about this question
When they act so cold
When they give up so easy
And you cared for them so much
And everything felt mutual
Maybe it even felt like they liked you more
And now it feels like they don't care about you at all
And you did nothing wrong
And you tried and tried
Was any of it real?

Maybe one day things will be different for you and I

After all
Growth is a powerful thing.

Pause

Continue

It felt like fireworks in the summer sky

Like sunshine on a Sunday morning
Like gentle rainfall on a cold night
But it also felt like
Chaos
Sadness
Despair
Everything came crashing down so quickly
I became numb
All the good faded into the background
And in the pitch black
All there was left
Was pain

I took the sweetest joy

In the simplest of things
I wish it were that easy to love you, too.

Don't ever hold back

In fear of being too much
You deserve an unwavering love
That cherishes every part of you
That can't get enough of you
A love that chases after you
Long after they've seen all of you

So I drop everything

And I search for you
To no avail once again
The *you* I knew
Has been gone far too long to ever be found.
Yet I try.

You gently whisper into my ear

"You look beautiful"
You gaze into my eyes
And your lips softly press mine
In that moment
The whole world disappears behind us
All that matters is you.
It's all that ever did.

When tears are streaming down your beautiful face

Your heart is aching
Your chest gets tight and you feel anxious
And you're questioning whether you should be with
them
That is your sign
That you shouldn't.
You know yourself best
And you're feeling this way for a reason
Don't think about the what-ifs
The hopes
The potential
The past
Look at the present.
Why is your heart residing where it does not feel safe?

It's strange that everyday things

Were just *things*
Until you came along
And intertwined little pieces of you
Into *everything*.
And I hate so much that you did that
Because you did not stay.
And now all I have
Are little reminders of you
In all of my surroundings
And I think
That may just be worse
Than not having you at all.

It took all of me to let go.

I'm so glad I finally did.

I wish I got to see you one more time

So we could share one more laugh
One more hug
One more kiss
So I could wrap my arms around you tightly and tell you
that I didn't want you to go
But I knew our end was inevitable
I could not prolong it any further
As much as my heart wanted to
My mind knew that I was falling
Falling into an abyss.

I don't want to admit
I always had a small glimmer of hope
That you'd be there to catch me.

Take the long way home today.

Knowing you

Was one of the most extraordinary things I've done
How life changing it is
When two imperfect souls
Connect the way ours did.
In your reflection
I saw myself
I knew myself for the first time.
As one
We were imperfectly perfect.

As long as we are lying to ourselves

We are trapped
Knowing no better than to stay in the comfort we
falsely created
Instead of facing the discomfort of reality.

I am trying my best to meet you where you need me

to meet you
I'm not sure if you'll still be in love with me by then.
Does love fade that quickly?
Do I worry too much?
Am I taking too long to figure it out?
Tell me you still love me.

We grew apart

And flourished into something
Far better
We were never meant for forever.

I'm still thinking about

Whether you ever think about me.

Forgive

Not for them
But for you
You will never be happy with yourself
If you have hate in your heart for others.

It was the way you lit up

Talking about your passions.

Tell me everything

Distance can be the greatest form of peace.

Take a step back if you need to

Don't rush yourself into a space
You are not ready to be in
It's okay to take things slow
It's okay if you're not where you thought you'd be by
now
You will get there when it's time, my love.

I called you today.

I know we decided
That we could not be together
As much as we wanted to be
And that we wouldn't call
That we wouldn't keep up on each other's lives
But my heart could never simply forget you
And go on like it never knew you
It desperately needed
To flutter once more
At the sound of your voice

Expecting things to be perfect

After you heal and finally feel good in
The space you find yourself
Is not realistic
Healing
Is a journey
We will have ups and downs
Moments where we feel bad about things
We thought we moved past
New things will break us down
But if we continue to grow
We will continue to overcome
We will do the best we can

Uncertainty

Surrounds every part
Of you and I
I just wish someone
Would finally *be sure*.

As I put my hand in yours

I could feel
Every butterfly fly away
You gave me a sense of calm
Like everything would be just fine
And for a while
It was hard to no longer have that
Some days
I genuinely needed it
But I learned to be that for myself.
I learned to be
A lot of things
For myself.

I'm sorry I can't give you the me

That's completely free
Trusting
Eager
The me that's a full-fledged lover
The me I was before I broke so many times

She's just a bit too naive
She loves too hard
Falls too quick

She shatters into a million pieces

I've gotten tired of cleaning up the mess.

I loved every piece of you

Your big brown eyes
Lighting up at the sight of me
Your gentle voice
Each word rolling off your tongue
Engraving themselves into the depths of my mind
Your winsome smile and your heavenly lips
Your soft hands floating into mine

I never thought I'd be letting you go.

We are all going through something

As small or significant as it may be.
Kindness goes a long way.

I hope you make someone smile today.

Buy yourself flowers

Compliment yourself
Tell yourself you can
Uplift yourself
You don't need anybody else
To do these things for you

We always focus on the good

Blurring the reason
We decided to leave
In the first place
Trust your instincts
The picture is clear

Rest. You need it, my love.

Your struggles are valid

Regardless of how they may look
In comparison
To others'.

It has been so hard

Relearning
To do every day
Without you.

My mind is mess enough.

I do not want a messy love.
I want my veins flowing with serenity
My fingertips grasping affection
My feet pacing on excitement
My heart racing with love
I want a love to set my soul on fire
And never let it burn out.
I want you to give me everything.
But please
Do not give me mess.

Follow your heart

But make sure your mind is at peace, too.

You come back

Expecting things to have stayed the same
It's too late, my love
I have moved on
Not with anybody else
But with myself
It was too late, the exact same moment you first left.

How can you seek shelter

In the same heart
You tore down.

I guess I just never understood

How it was so easy for you
To let it all go.

If they aren't trying

Why are you?
Regardless of everything else
It's as simple as that, my love.

Erase it from your mind

That they might come back.

Love yourself.

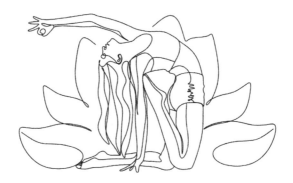

End~

To all who I've shared my heart with, it's all love. While each one turned out to be a lesson, I'm glad I was able to have these experiences and receive and give love. I'm glad I was able to grow from these experiences and find myself. I will always know my worth, sometimes my kindness gets in the way of that, but I will always find my way.

To my bestest friend, whom I've shared so many of these experiences with, whom I've cried to and been a shoulder to cry on for, I love you. You've helped me through so much in life and are such a large part of who I am today. Thank you— you deserve the world. I hope these poems serve as a reminder to you.

To the readers, thank you for listening to my stories. I truly hope you could find something to take away from them. Lead with love, always.

Line art credits: